LEGAL & HUMBLE AI

Addressing the Legal, Ethical, and Societal Dilemmas of Generative AI

genitive AEQUITATIS

By David King

INGENE
PUBLISHERS™
MARKET.SELL.PUBLISH

A division of the Ingene Group
ISBN: 978-1-909524-99-6

Web: www.legalandhumbleai.com
Email: ingenepublishers@gmail.com

Printed in the United Kingdom.
Marketed & distributed by
Ingene Publications,
63 Fernhead road
Maida Vale, W9
London.

Contents

Preface

Legal and Humble AI
Addressing the Legal, Ethical, and Societal Dilemmas of Generative AI

A next revolution is nigh. It is brewing in the depths of code and algorithms. Generative AI, the enigmatic force behind captivating narratives, exquisite paintings, and lifelike melodies, is reshaping our world before our very eyes. Its potential to unlock unimaginable creative vistas is as undeniable as the ethical labyrinth it weaves. In this burgeoning era of digital alchemy, we stand at a crossroads. Do we embrace the boundless possibilities offered by this technological muse, or do we recoil from the unforeseen consequences it may spawn? This book is a clarion call, a map through the ethical maze, a necessary dialogue not just for tech pundits but for every citizen.

Generative AI's applications transcend the realm of artistic dalliance. From revolutionizing healthcare with personalized medical diagnoses to tailoring education to individual learning styles, its tentacles reach into every facet of human experience. Imagine surgeons trained on simulated surgeries performed by virtual patients, or courtroom trials aided by AI-powered evidence analysis. Yet, within these transformative promises lurk shadows of legal and ethical quandaries.

What happens when AI-generated art plagiarizes human artistry? Who bears the legal responsibility for a self-driving car's accident? Does a generative algorithm deserve copyright protection for its creations? These are not mere hypotheticals; they are the pressing concerns demanding immediate attention.

This book delves deep into these uncharted territories, navigating the treacherous waters of intellectual property, liability, and algorithmic bias. We examine the UK's Copyright, Designs and Patents Act 1988, Data Protection Act 2018, and Automated and Electric Vehicles Act 2018, seeking legal frameworks that can accommodate this unprecedented phenomenon.

But legality is just one piece of the puzzle. Ethical considerations – the spectre of job displacement, the potential for discriminatory algorithms, and the erosion of human agency – necessitate a deeper philosophical reflection. This is where the concept of "Humble AI," becomes relevant. It is a philosophy in some sections of the technological world that proposes a framework advocating for transparency, accountability, and a constant vigil against algorithmic overreach.

Introduction

Artificial intelligence (AI) has become an integral part of our daily lives, from virtual assistants to self-driving cars. However, as AI technology advances, it raises legal, ethical, and societal dilemmas that must be addressed. One area of AI that has garnered attention is generative AI, which involves machines creating original content such as music, art, and literature. The legal challenges posed by generative AI are complex and require a multidisciplinary approach".[1] This means developing framework that involve experts in law, computer science, ethics, and philosophy. According to Floridi and Sanders, the development of AI will require collaboration from different fields. By involving a diverse range of stakeholder, policymakers can gain a more comprehensive understanding of the social, ethical, and legal implications of generative AI.[2] This can help to ensure that regulatory frameworks are responsive to the needs and concerns of all stakeholders, and that they promote the development of safe, trustworthy, and socially beneficial AI systems.

---

1 Mireille Hildebrandt and Kieron O'Hara (eds), *Life and the Law in the Era of Data-Driven Agency* (Edward Elgar Publishing 2020).

2 Markus Dirk Dubber, Frank Pasquale and Sunit Das, *The Oxford Handbook of Ethics of AI* (Oxford university press 2020).

One example of a regulatory framework that aims to promote the development of safe and trustworthy AI systems is the European Union's General Data Protection Regulation (GDPR). The GDPR includes provisions that require transparency and accountability in the use of AI, as well as safeguards for individuals' privacy and data protection .[3] By prioritizing the needs and concerns of all stakeholders, including individuals and organizations, the GDPR can help to ensure that AI systems are developed in a responsible and ethical manner.

A survey conducted by the European Union Agency for Fundamental Rights found that 71% of companies reported that the GDPR4 had a positive effect on their AI projects, with 64% stating that it helped to increase trust in their systems. [5]This highlights the importance of data protection regulations in ensuring that AI is developed and used in a responsible and ethical manner, ultimately benefiting both individuals and organizations.

This emphasis on responsible AI development and deployment is not unique to Europe. In fact, a study conducted by the Stanford Institute for Human-Centered

---

3 'GDPR_FINAL_EPSU.Pdf' <https://www.epsu.org/sites/default/files/article/files/GDPR_FINAL_EPSU.pdf> accessed 13 February 2024.

4 'Regulation - 2016/679 - EN - Gdpr - EUR-Lex' <https://eur-lex.europa.eu/eli/reg/2016/679/oj> accessed 21 February 2024. [1]'

5 'Getting the Future Right – Artificial Intelligence and Fundamental Rights' (*European Union Agency for Fundamental Rights*, 18 November 2020) <http://fra.europa.eu/en/publication/2020/artificial-intelligence-and-fundamental-rights> accessed 13 February 2024.

Artificial Intelligence found that ethical considerations are becoming increasingly important in the development of AI systems worldwide.[6]

As AI continues to advance and become more integrated into our daily lives, it is crucial that we prioritize ethical principles and human values in its design and use. This is especially important given the potential for AI to perpetuate existing biases and inequalities, as well as create new ones. As noted by Buolamwini and Gebru [7], biased data sets can lead to biased algorithms, which can have harmful consequences for marginalized communities. Therefore, it is essential that we actively work to identify and address these biases in AI systems.

One example of the harmful consequences of biased algorithms is in the criminal justice system. A study by Dressel and Farid [8] found that a widely used algorithm for predicting recidivism was biased against black defendants, leading to higher rates of false positives and false negatives for this group. This highlights the urgent need for ongoing monitoring and evaluation of AI

6 'Ai_index_2019_report.Pdf' <https://hai.stanford.edu/sites/default/files/ai_index_2019_report.pdf> accessed 13 February 2024.

7 Joy Buolamwini and Timnit Gebru, 'Gender Shades: Intersectional Accuracy Disparities in Commercial Gender Classification', *Proceedings of the 1st Conference on Fairness, Accountability and Transparency* (PMLR 2018) <https://proceedings.mlr.press/v81/buolamwini18a.html> accessed 13 February 2024.

8 Julia Dressel and Hany Farid, 'The Accuracy, Fairness, and Limits of Predicting Recidivism' (2018) 4 Science Advances eaao5580.

systems to ensure they are fair and just. As Buolamwini and Gebru[9] argue, it is not enough to simply acknowledge the existence of bias; we must actively work to address it.

9 Buolamwini and Gebru (n 10).

Chapter ONE

The Power and Peril of Generative AI alongside the ethical landmines.

Generative AI, or artificial intelligence that can create original content, has the potential to revolutionize the creative industries. From music and literature to visual art and advertising, AI-generated content has already made its mark. However, this new technology has revealed gaps in our legal system including having dire impact on societal cohesion as it can create polarisation of views.

Recent studies have shown that the use of artificial intelligence (AI) in healthcare can improve patient outcomes and reduce costs . AI system can assist healthcare professionals in making more accurate diagnoses, predicting patient outcomes, and identifying potential health risks before they become serious. However, there are also concerns about the ethical implications of using AI in healthcare, such as issues related to privacy and bias . This may have impact on the doctor-patient relationship. Patients may feel uncomfortable sharing personal information with a machine, and there is a risk that AI could replace human interaction altogether.[10]. Additionally, there are concerns about the accuracy of AI algorithms, particularly when it comes to marginalized populations who may not be adequately represented in the data used to train these systems[11]. As such, it is important for healthcare professionals to carefully consider the ethical implications of using AI and work to mitigate any potential harms.

One of the most significant ethical implications of AI-generated content is the potential for it to be used to deceive or manipulate people. For example, AI-generated news articles or social media posts could be used to spread false information or propaganda. Additionally, there is concern that AI-generated content could be used to create deepfakes, or manipulated videos that appear to be real. This could have serious consequences for individuals and society.

Another concern is the potential for AI-generated content to perpetuate bias and discrimination. If the algorithms used to create the content are biased, this bias will be reflected in the output. For example, an AI-generated resume screening tool could inadvertently discriminate against certain groups of people if the algorithm is trained on biased data. It is important to consider these potential consequences and

---

10 Thomas Davenport and Ravi Kalakota, 'The Potential for Artificial Intelligence in Healthcare' (2019) 6 Future Healthcare Journal 94.

11 Ziad Obermeyer and others, 'Dissecting Racial Bias in an Algorithm Used to Manage the Health of Populations' (2019) 366 Science 447.

ensure that AI-generated content is developed in an ethical and responsible manner.

Determining ownership and attribution in AI-generated art and literature can be challenging. If an algorithm creates a piece of art or literature, who owns the copyright? Additionally, how can attribution be given if there was no human involvement in the creation process?

The potential consequences of not properly attributing AI-generated content are significant. For example, if an AI algorithm creates a piece of music that becomes popular, it may be difficult to determine who should receive credit and royalties for its creation. It is important to consider these challenges and develop systems for properly attributing ownership and authorship in AI-generated content. For example, some musicians are using AI algorithms to create new songs or remix existing ones. Additionally, some authors are using AI algorithms to generate plot ideas or even entire novels.

The potential consequences of AI-generated content on traditional creative industries are complex. On one hand, it could lead to new forms of creativity and innovation. On the other hand, it could lead to job loss or a devaluation of human creativity. It is important to consider these potential consequences and ensure that traditional creative industries are not negatively impacted by the rise of AI-generated content.

The Future of Copyright Law in the Age of AI.

As AI-generated content becomes more prevalent, copyright law is evolving to account for these new forms of creativity. For example, some countries have already granted copyright protection to works created by algorithms.

AI-generated content has significant potential for use in advertising and marketing campaigns. For example, an algorithm could generate personalized ads based on a user's browsing history or social media activity.

However, there is concern that this technology could be used for unethical purposes such as manipulating consumer behaviour or spreading false information. It is important for advertisers and marketers to consider these ethical implications and ensure that their use of AI-generated content is responsible and transparent.

The Potential for AI-generated Content to Mislead and Manipulate.

AI-generated content that mislead or manipulate people are also a concern. For example, deepfakes could be used to create videos that appear to show someone saying or doing something they did not actually do.

The consequences of this type of manipulation could be significant, both on an individual level and on a societal level. It is important for developers and users of AI-generated content to consider these potential consequences and ensure that their use of this technology does not contribute to deception or manipulation.

The Responsibility of AI Creators and Developers to Consider Ethical Implications.

Creators and developers of AI bear a profound responsibility to society when creating AI systems. A responsible creator of AI should weave into the very fabric of their creations the principle of "Humble AI". This should begin with a commitment to transparency, ensuring that the inner workings of AI systems are comprehensible and accessible to all stakeholders. By demystifying the technology, creators empower users to engage critically and responsibly with AI, fostering a culture of informed decision-making.

Overall, the rise of generative AI has brought about a new era of creativity, with endless possibilities for art, literature, and music. However, as with any new technology, there are ethical implications that must be considered. The use of AI-generated content raises questions about ownership, attribution, and bias, as well as the potential for manipulation and deception in advertising and marketing. While there are certainly risks associated with generative AI in creative industries, there are also many potential benefits. It is up to us as a society to carefully consider these ethical implications and work towards finding solutions that balance these risks and benefits. By doing so, we can ensure that generative AI is used in a way that promotes creativity, innovation, and social good.

Chapter TWO

Societal Impact and Public Perception.

Public perceptions of generative AI are varied and often shaped by a combination of fascination and trepidation. Addressing both the positive and negative aspects is vital. Issues such as job displacement, loss of privacy, and the potential for misuse. Questions regarding AI bias, and the human-machine relationship will require ongoing public discourse and robust ethical frameworks to ensure responsible and equitable development.

Society will require a cultural shift to adapt to these technologies and a new narrative will be needed towards influencing public opinion.

It is worth noting, that technology is not neutral. It reflects our values, our biases, and our choices. In the hands of responsible developers and informed users, generative AI can be a powerful tool for progress. But if we succumb to complacency and ignore the ethical challenges, we risk unleashing a Pandora's box of societal ills. We must strive for a future where AI augments our humanity, not undermines it, where creativity becomes a bridge, not a weapon, and where ethical considerations reign supreme in the digital realm we are co-creating.

The ever-evolving landscape of generative AI's impact on society is both profound and multifaceted. Generative AI in the realms of employment, education, and social media creates a social dynamic, one that most of us are not prepared for. Additionally, the fast pace of AI creates a complex web of public perceptions, fears, and expectations that accompany the integration of these transformative technologies.

Social Media.

The impact of social media on society has been extensively studied by researchers. A study conducted by Pew Research Center found that 69% of adults in the United States use social media, with Facebook being the most popular platform.[12] The study also revealed that social media has become a primary source of news and information for many people, with 43% of adults getting their news from Facebook.[13] This highlights the significant role that social media plays in shaping public opinion and influencing

---

12 'Privacy Management Among Social Media Natives: An Exploratory Study of Facebook and Snapchat - Erin E. Hollenbaugh, 2019' <https://journals.sagepub.com/doi/full/10.1177/2056305119855144> accessed 16 February 2024.

13 ibid.

societal trends. As social media continues to evolve, it is likely that its impact on society will only continue to grow.

Social media has also been a tool in the democratic process. In a recent Netflix's documentary "The Great Hack" which narrated how Cambridge Analytica and its parent company, SCL Group, manipulated elections worldwide.[14] The company used millions of people's data without consent for political campaigns, including Trump's 2016 presidential bid and Brexit's Leave Campaign. [15]In Trinidad and Tobago, the company influenced voting behaviour, working for the majority-Indian United National Congress party and smaller affiliate parties. The campaign, "Do So," aimed to increase apathy among young, black voters, interpreting their refusal to vote as resistance against politics. The UNC ultimately won the 2010 election using this tactic.[16]

Recent studies have shown link between excessive social media use and increased mental health issues. Negative mental health outcomes such as depression, anxiety, and low self-esteem. [17]This emphasizes the importance of

---

14 'Netflix's "The Great Hack" Highlights Cambridge Analytica's Role in Trinidad & Tobago Elections' (*Global Voices Advox*, 6 August 2019) <https://advox.globalvoices.org/2019/08/06/netflixs-the-great-hack-highlights-cambridge-analyticas-role-in-trinidad-tobago-elections/> accessed 13 February 2024.

15 ibid

16 ibid

17 Kuan-Yu Lin and Hsi-Peng Lu, 'Why People Use Social Networking Sites: An Empirical Study Integrating Network Externalities and Motivation Theory' (2011) 27 Computers in Human Behavior 1152.

monitoring our social media habits and finding a healthy balance between online and offline activities. As we become more aware of the potential risks associated with social media, it is crucial for individuals and society to take proactive steps towards responsible usage.

Employment Landscape in the Age of Generative AI.

The introduction of generative AI has significantly altered the employment landscape, raising questions about the nature of work, job security, and the distribution of economic opportunities. Automation, driven by generative AI, has led to the displacement of certain jobs while creating new avenues for skilled workers. The societal implications of these changes including the potential for economic inequality and the need for adaptive education and training programs are all concerns that has been thrust on society.

According to a report by the World Economic report Forum [18], "by 2022, no less than 54% of all employees will require significant re-skilling and upskilling" due to the impact of AI on the workforce. Repetitive, data-driven tasks face high automation potential. Clerical, manufacturing, and transportation jobs are particularly vulnerable.

18 'The Future of Jobs Report 2018' (*World Economic Forum*) <https://www.weforum.org/publications/the-future-of-jobs-report-2018/> accessed 13 February 2024.

Furthermore, the impact of AI on the workforce is not limited to job displacement and the need for new skills. It also raises ethical concerns about the use of AI in decision-making processes, such as hiring and lending. This can have dire consequences if the data is skewed or unreliable. Biases in data and algorithms can perpetuate discrimination and inequality, leading to a lack of diversity in the workplace and society. As AI becomes more prevalent in our daily lives, it is crucial to address these ethical concerns and ensure that AI is developed and used in a responsible and equitable manner. [19]

Redefining Work: The Emergence of New Professions.

As AI continues to advance, many jobs will be displaced. However, this does not necessarily mean that there will be a net loss of jobs. In fact, some experts predict that AI will create new jobs and industries that we cannot even imagine yet. According to a report by the World Economic Forum, "The Future of Jobs 2018," it is estimated that by 2022, 75 million jobs may be displaced by AI, but 133 million new jobs may be created.[20] This suggests that while there will be significant changes in the job market, there is also

19 'The Ethics of Algorithms: Mapping the Debate - Brent Daniel Mittelstadt, Patrick Allo, Mariarosaria Taddeo, Sandra Wachter, Luciano Floridi, 2016' <https://journals.sagepub.com/doi/full/10.1177/2053951716679679> accessed 13 February 2024.

20 'The Future of Jobs Report 2018' (n 20).

potential for growth and innovation. Job displacement could be offset by job creation in some other sectors. For example, AI jobs such as development, maintenance, and ethical oversight could become career paths. This will be most noticeable in the health sector.[21]

As stated in the report[22], there is a shift towards jobs that require more cognitive and social skills, as well as creativity and problem-solving abilities .[23] This means that individuals will need to adapt and acquire new skills to remain competitive in the job market. With this novel job roles, it is important to emphasise the importance of adaptability and upskilling.

Re-skilling and Upskilling.

According to a report by the World Economic Forum, re-skilling and upskilling programs will be critical in preparing the workforce for the jobs of the future.[24]

These programs not only benefit individual workers, but also contribute to the overall economic growth of a country.

21 'The Future of Jobs Report 2018' (*World Economic Forum*) <https://www.weforum.org/publications/the-future-of-jobs-report-2018/> accessed 13 February 2024.

22 ibid.

23 'The Future of Work: How New Technologies Are Transforming Tasks' (*MIT-IBM Watson AI Lab*) <https://mitibmwatsonailab.mit.edu/research/blog/the-future-of-work-how-new-technologies-are-transforming-tasks/> accessed 13 February 2024.

24 'The Future of Jobs Report 2018' (n 20).

A study conducted by the Organisation for Economic Co-operation and Development (OECD) found that investing in adult learning and training can lead to increased productivity, higher wages, and reduced unemployment rates.[25] Therefore, re-skilling, and upskilling programs should be a priority for governments and businesses alike to ensure a skilled workforce that can adapt to the changing demands of the job market.

Adapting to the AI-driven world will require continuous learning. Educational systems must prioritize critical thinking, adaptability, collaboration, and digital literacy to equip individuals with skills that complement, not compete with, AI.

Gig Economy Expansion.

The gig economy has been expanding rapidly in recent years, and the rise of artificial intelligence (AI) is likely to accelerate this trend. According to a study by McKinsey Global Institute, up to 375 million workers worldwide may need to switch occupational categories and learn new skills by 2030 due to automation and AI.[26]. This means

25 OECD, 'An OECD Learning Framework 2030' in Gerald Bast, Elias G Carayannis and David FJ Campbell (eds), *The Future of Education and Labor* (Springer International Publishing 2019) <https://doi.org/10.1007/978-3-030-26068-2_3> accessed 13 February 2024.

26 James Manyika and others, 'Jobs Lost, Jobs Gained: What the Future of Work Will Mean for Jobs, Skills, and Wages' (McKinsey Global Institute 2017) Report <https://apo.org.au/node/199751> accessed 13 February 2024.

that more people may turn to gig work to earn income and adapt to the changing job market. As AI continues to advance, it will create new opportunities for gig workers in areas such as data annotation, virtual assistance, and content moderation. As such, the gig economy is likely to play an increasingly important role in shaping the future of work.

Laws could be enacted that make these kinds of jobs more secure since they are here to stay.

Educational Paradigms.

Generative AI has begun to permeate educational systems, offering innovative tools for personalized learning and content creation. However, concerns arise regarding the ethical use of AI in education, student privacy, and the potential for exacerbating educational inequalities. The transformative potential of generative AI in education necessitates an ethical guideline to ensure its responsible integration.

The following are its potential uses.

Personalized Learning: AI-powered tutors and adaptive learning platforms can personalize education, catering to individual strengths and weaknesses. This raises concerns about equity and access to technology, necessitating inclusive educational models.

Lifelong Learning: Education will no longer be confined to classrooms or fixed stages of life. AI can facilitate continuous learning and skill development throughout one's career and personal journey.

Focus on Skill Development: Curriculums must shift towards practical skills development, preparing individuals for real-world applications of knowledge and problem-solving in collaboration with AI tools.

Bridging the Gap: Communicating AI's Societal Impact.

To mitigate fears and align expectations, citizen's participation and effective communication is paramount. There should be transparent communication from developers, policymakers, and educators in shaping public perceptions. Strategies for fostering an informed and engaged public, emphasizing the need for open dialogue to address concerns and build trust in the transformative power of generative AI.

It is crucial to strike a balance between technological progress and the well-being of individuals and communities. Contributing to the ongoing discourse surrounding the transformative technologies, providing insights into the societal dynamics and public perceptions that will shape the future of generative AI's integration.

As societies embrace automation, maintaining a human-centric approach becomes paramount. It is important to stress that the design and release of technology into society must occur in the following sequence. Firstly, consideration must be given to the impact on society. Secondly, there must be a stipulation that all technology should enhance human well-being rather than disrupt it. Finally, there should be emphasis on collaboration between technology developers, policymakers, and the workforce.

Societal Adaptation and Safety Nets.

To navigate the jobless future, societies must adapt. Job displacement due to automation is a global phenomenon, but its impact varies across different regions and cultures. We propose a comparative analysis, examining how various countries are grappling with the challenges of automation, the strategies they employ, and the lessons that can be learned from diverse approaches.

The relationship between work, identity, and meaning making will need to be redefined. Social safety nets and support systems will become crucial to navigate the changing social landscape.

Safety Nets

Universal Basic Income.

As automation disrupts traditional employment, safety nets such as universal basic income may be necessary to ensure that those who are displaced by AI are not left behind.[27] The concept of UBI is to ensure basic needs are met and individuals can pursue more fulfilling work or creative endeavours.

Namibia: In 2021, Namibia piloted a two-year UBI program in two rural communities. The program provided a monthly stipend to all residents regardless of employment status and achieved positive results in terms of food security and well-being.

Finland: Between 2017 and 2018, Finland conducted a two-year experiment providing unemployed individuals with a basic income. While the program did not show significant changes in employment rates, it did improve mental well-being and reduce financial stress among participants.

Kenya: In 2017, Kenya launched a UBI pilot in several villages focusing on improving food security and economic opportunities for residents. The program demonstrated positive impacts on poverty reduction and child nutrition.

27 Stuart Russell and Peter Norvig, *Artificial Intelligence: A Modern Approach, Global Edition* (3rd edition, Pearson 2016).

Stockholm, Sweden: A two-year UBI pilot is currently underway in Stockholm, involving hundreds of randomly selected residents receiving a monthly stipend. This program will gather data on the impact of UBI on factors like employment, health, and overall well-being.

Chapter THREE

The legal and ethical quandaries surrounding intellectual property, AI-generated works, and autonomous robots.

As generative AI sips into every creative space, the UK legal landscape grapples with the challenge of weaving a regulatory framework strong enough to contain its potential and flexible enough to nurture its growth. In this chapter, we explore the existing statutes and regulations that touch upon this new frontier.

GDPR: At the heart of the dance between data and AI lies the General Data Protection Regulation (GDPR).[28] This robust piece of legislation grants individuals significant control over their personal information, demanding transparency, and accountability from all who process it. Generative AI, with its insatiable appetite for data, falls squarely under the GDPR's purview. The very training data upon which AI thrives might inadvertently contain personal information, triggering the regulation's complex web of data protection principles. The question then arises: can AI-generated

28 'Regulation - 2016/679 - EN - Gdpr - EUR-Lex' (n 3).

outputs – be it a personalized musical composition or a bespoke medical textbook – be considered personal data protected by the GDPR? This is a legal riddle awaiting a Solomon-like judgment.

The Data Protection Act: Flanking the GDPR in the UK is the Data Protection Act 2018.[29] This act, pre-dating the GDPR, serves as a complementary pillar in the data protection edifice. It emphasizes principles like accountability, fairness, and purpose limitation, all of which find direct application to the realm of generative AI. For instance, the Act's emphasis on transparency demands that developers disclose the use of generative AI in their applications, allowing users to make informed choices about their data's fate.

Copyright Conundrums: Stepping away from data protection, we examine the thorny thicket of copyright law enshrined in "The Copyright, Designs and Patents Act 1988" this legislation defines the legal parameters of artistic ownership, but its framework struggles to accommodate the nuances of AI-generated creations.

Does the author of the AI code deserve the copyright, or should it belong to the algorithm itself, or perhaps the human who provided the initial creative prompt? These are not simply philosophical quandaries; they have real-

29 Data Protection Act 2018' <https://www.legislation.gov.uk/ukpga/2018/12/contents/enacted> accessed 21 February 2024.

world consequences for artists and AI developers alike. Imagine a scenario where an AI-generated painting garners critical acclaim and financial success – who lays claim to the royalties? The law should evolve to embrace the idea of AI authorship until then, these questions will remain vexing enigmas.

While the GDPR, Data Protection Act, and Copyright Act provide a baseline for regulating AI, their limitations are becoming increasingly apparent. The UK Government, recognizing the need for a more targeted approach, has published a white paper advocating for a "pro-innovation, proportionate, trustworthy, adaptable, clear and collaborative" framework for AI regulation. This promising approach, still in its infancy, seeks to empower existing regulators – like the Information Commissioner's Office (ICO) – to develop sector-specific guidance for AI applications, including generative AI. However, critics have argued that this can be rigid, fragmented, have limited scope, complex and lack consensus.

We propose instead one singular measuring line in all AI systems that involves Ethical Principles, Risk Assessment, Regulatory Guidelines such as human-centred design, Stakeholder Engagement, Education and Training and Monitoring and Evaluation.

The Road Ahead: Building a Bridge, not a Wall.

The legal landscape surrounding generative AI in the UK is a dynamic and evolving space. As technology marches forward, the law must dance nimbly alongside it, adapting to its ever-changing rhythms. The roadmap for navigating this thrilling and perilous terrain are not merely academic exercises; they are the threads with which we will weave this looming technological future which will allow us to flourish and for the technology to become legal and humble.

As we navigate this uncharted legal territory, it is crucial to acknowledge that regulations should not stifle innovation. The answer lies not in erecting rigid walls around generative AI, but in building bridges of trust and understanding. A collaborative approach, involving developers, legal experts, and the public, is essential to develop a regulatory framework that fosters responsible AI development while safeguarding individual rights and societal well-being.

The Driverless Dilemma: Responsibility in the Age of Automation.

The emergence of self-driving cars has brought to the forefront a complex and thorny issue: legal liability in accidents involving these autonomous systems. The challenges, legal frameworks, and ethical considerations surrounding accidents involving self-driving cars.

In the UK, the highway code holds human drivers to a particular standard. Below are specific legislations and case laws that cover the following:

Negligence: Road users owe a duty of care to others on the road. Negligence claims may arise from actions that breach this duty, causing harm or damage.

Personal Injury Claims: If a road user is injured due to the negligence of another, they may have a claim for personal injury.

Property Damage Claims: Damage to property (vehicles, for example) caused by the negligence of another driver may lead to a property damage claim.

Public Liability: Authorities or individuals responsible for road maintenance may be liable for accidents caused by poorly maintained roads.

Manufacturer Liability: In cases where a defect in the vehicle contributes to an accident, the manufacturer may be held liable.

Legislation

- **Road Traffic Act 1988:** This act sets out general driving rules and obligations, including the requirement to "drive with due care and attention." While not explicitly stating a duty of care, it lays the foundation for negligence claims by establishing expected standards of behaviour on the road.

- **Highways Act 1980:** This act places responsibilities on authorities for maintaining highways in a safe condition. Failure to meet these responsibilities can lead to public liability claims if accidents occur due to poor road maintenance.

Case Law:

Donoghue v Stevenson (1932)[30]*:* This landmark case established the "neighbour principle," which posits that a duty of care exists when foreseeable harm could be caused by one person's actions to another. This principle is crucial in proving negligence in road accidents, as it helps determine whether the driver owed a duty of care to the injured party.

Nettleship v Weston (1991) [31]*:* This case clarified the "reasonable driver" standard. It established that the duty of care owed by road users is to act as a "reasonably prudent and competent driver" in the circumstances. This standard

30 *Donoghue v Stevenson [1932] UKHL 100* (UKHL (1932)).

31 *Nettleship v Weston [1971] EWCA Civ 6* (EWCA (Civ)).

is used to assess whether a driver breached their duty and caused harm.

Montgomery v Lanarkshire Health Board (2015[32]***):*** This case introduced the concept of "reasonable foreseeability" in personal injury claims. It stated that a duty of care exists only if the harm caused was both a real and substantial risk, not just a mere possibility. This can be relevant in road accidents where, determining foreseeability of harm, especially to third parties, is important.

Legal Frameworks and Jurisdictional Challenges.

As self-driving cars operate across different jurisdictions, legal frameworks become a critical aspect of addressing liability issues. The existing legal frameworks, both internationally and within specific countries, that attempt to establish responsibility in cases of accidents involving autonomous vehicles. In the UK, applying the Highway Code and the Road Traffic Act maybe relevant legal references but are they fit for purpose?

Currently, the legal framework for AVs remains a patchwork quilt, stitched together from regulations designed for human drivers and vehicles. The Road Traffic Act 1988 holds drivers responsible for their actions on the road.

32 *Montgomery v Lanarkshire Health Board [2015] UKSC 11* (UKSC (2015)).

But who shoulders the blame when the wheel belongs to an algorithm? Is it the manufacturer, the programmer, or perhaps the passenger enjoying a hands-free journey? This conundrum lies at the heart of the legal and ethical quandary surrounding AVs.

To navigate this legal maze, governments worldwide are scrambling to adapt existing regulations and draft new ones specifically for AVs. The UK's Automated and Electric Vehicles Act 2018 marks a significant step, recognizing the concept of automated driving and assigning responsibility to the "keeper" of thc AV in the event of accidents. However, questions remain about the "keeper's" degree of liability and the potential for loopholes in complex ownership structures. For example, how liability would be determined in the cases of the 5 levels of automated vehicles.[33]

Beyond the legal complexities, AVs raise ethical dilemmas requiring careful consideration. For example, in "*Trolley problems*" – those hypothetical scenarios where an AV must choose between harming one person or another – challenge us to define how such vehicles should prioritize safety in unavoidable collisions. Moreover, the potential for algorithmic bias to creep into AV decision-making, like prioritizing certain demographics in pedestrian avoidance scenarios, poses serious ethical concerns that must be

33 'What Are Autonomous Car Levels? Levels 1 to 5 of Driverless Vehicle Tech Explained' (CAR Magazine) <https://www.carmagazine.co.uk/car-news/tech/autonomous-car-levels-different-driverless-technology-levels-explained/> accessed 21 February 2024.

addressed. The challenge of regulating AVs is not singular; it demands international cooperation to ensure harmonized standards and avoid regulatory fragmentation. Initiatives like the Vienna Convention on Road Traffic, currently undergoing revisions to incorporate automation, serve as stepping stones towards a cohesive global framework.

The Gray Area: Ethical Considerations in Algorithmic Decision-Making.

The line between human control and machine autonomy becomes blurred in self-driving cars, leading to questions about human-machine interaction and supervision. This section explores the role of human drivers in autonomous vehicles, examining the challenges and legal implications when humans need to take control in critical situations.

As self-driving cars rely on intricate algorithms to make split-second decisions, ethical considerations come to the forefront. Ethical dimensions of algorithmic decision-making in autonomous vehicles such as prioritization of safety, potential biases, and the responsibility of developers in shaping these algorithms.

To address the challenges the following solutions are proposed namely.

Testing and Certification: Establishing procedures for testing and certifying autonomous vehicle technologies ensures they meet safety standards before being deployed on public roads.

Infrastructure Upgrades: Adapting infrastructure, such as roads and traffic signals, to accommodate autonomous vehicles can improve safety and efficiency.

Product Liability Laws: Clarifying liability in the event of accidents involving autonomous vehicles is crucial. An example of liability Legal framework could be that the manufacturers, software developers, and vehicle operators will be jointly and severally liable.

Insurance Policies: Insurance companies should consider adapting policies to account for the shift in liability from human drivers to manufacturers and software developers of autonomous systems.

Generative AI isn't just playing in the realm of art and music; it's infiltrating real-world decisions with profound ethical implications. Below are three case studies that illustrate the potential conflicts between AI's dazzling potential and our human moral compass.

Algorithmic Bias: The insidious dangers of biased in the Justice system.

In 2019, a US criminal risk assessment tool, heavily reliant on AI algorithms, was found to be racially biased, unfairly assigning higher recidivism risk scores to Black defendants.[34] This case illustrates the ethical pitfalls of relying on black-box algorithms for critical decisions like sentencing. Without transparency and rigorous audits, AI can perpetuate real-world inequalities hidden within its training data and code. We must demand open algorithms, accountable developers, and diverse datasets to ensure AI systems don't exacerbate existing societal biases. We could also develop an AI model that corrects the disparities in sentencing.

The Weaponisation of Creativity: When AI Fuels Harmful Narratives.

In 2023, an AI-powered writing tool generated a fictional story riddled with misogynistic and racist tropes.[35] While quickly retracted, this incident showcased the potential for AI to weaponize creativity, inadvertently generating harmful content. Who in law should be the reasonable person liable for such outputs – the developers, the users, or the algorithms themselves? This case highlights the need for ethical guidelines and human oversight in generative

34 'Report on Algorithmic Risk Assessment Tools in the U.S. Criminal Justice System' (*Partnership on AI*, 23 April 2019) <https://partnershiponai.org/paper/report-on-machine-learning-in-risk-assessment-tools-in-the-u-s-criminal-justice-system/> accessed 16 February 2024.

35 Marie Lamensch, 'Generative AI Tools Are Perpetuating Harmful Gender Stereotypes' (*Centre for International Governance Innovation*) <https://www.cigionline.org/articles/generative-ai-tools-are-perpetuating-harmful-gender-stereotypes/> accessed 16 February 2024.

AI development, ensuring that creativity remains a force for good, not a tool for perpetuating prejudice.

Deepfakes: Blurring the Lines of Reality.

Imagine a news clip where a political leader appears to be making inflammatory statements they never uttered. This wasn't science fiction; it was the reality of the mayor of London , where a deepfake audio of him was used to spread misinformation and almost led to serious social disorder.[36] Deepfakes, hyper-realistic videos and audios generated by AI, raise terrifying ethical questions. Can we trust our eyes and ears in the digital age? How can we safeguard against malicious deepfakes manipulating public opinion and eroding trust in institutions? As AI tools become more sophisticated, the line between truth and fabricated reality grows thinner, demanding robust countermeasures and critical media literacy in a society bombarded by digital information.

While deepfakes raise concerns about misinformation and misuse, they also hold significant potential for positive applications within GAN (Generative Adversarial Network) architecture - where artificial data are generated to make up for lack of data where the output could have great benefits such as in robotic health care.

36 'Sadiq Khan Says Fake AI Audio of Him Nearly Led to Serious Disorder' *BBC News* (13 February 2024) <https://www.bbc.com/news/uk-68146053> accessed 16 February 2024.

Example of positive uses of Deep Fake.

Interactive Learning: Deepfakes can create personalized educational experiences with virtual tutors or historical figures explaining complex concepts in engaging ways. Imagine Shakespeare himself teaching his plays or Galileo Galilei demonstrating his telescope.

Accessibility Improvement: Deepfakes can translate sign language or foreign languages in real-time, making knowledge and educational resources accessible to a wider audience.

Immersive Learning: GANs can generate realistic simulations of historical events or scientific phenomena, allowing students to virtually experience events like the French Revolution or the workings of the human body.

Art and Creative Expression.

Collaborative Art Creation:

GANs can facilitate collaboration between artists, generating new styles and forms of creative expression. Imagine a painter using a GAN to create variations on their style or a musician collaborating with a virtual composer.

Preserving Cultural Heritage:

Deepfakes can help restore damaged historical recordings or recreate lost artworks, bringing the past back to life and preserving cultural heritage for future generations.

Personalized Storytelling:

GANs can personalize storylines or generate custom characters, enhancing the interactive experience of movies, games, or virtual reality narratives.

When AI Goes Too Far - Examples of Overstepping Boundaries.

The promise of AI is vast, with potential to revolutionize various aspects of life. However, like any powerful tool, it can be misused.

AI must be regulated and if not, we will keep seeing instances of the technology overstepping ethical and legal boundaries. These oversteps should serve as cautionary tales for responsible development and deployment.

The following are instances where AI oversteps boundaries.

1. Deepfakes for Malicious Intent:

Deepfake technology, while initially hailed for creative purposes, has morphed into a tool for misinformation and manipulation. Fabricated videos of politicians or celebrities making false statements can sow discord and undermine trust in public discourse.

2. Algorithmic Bias in Hiring and Credit Scoring:

Biases inherent in training data can seep into AI algorithms, leading to discriminatory outcomes in hiring, loan approvals, or criminal justice predictions. These biases, often reflecting societal prejudices, can perpetuate inequalities and harm individuals.

3. Social Scoring Systems in China:

China's social scoring system, which tracks and rates citizens based on behaviour and social media activity, raises concerns about privacy, freedom of expression, and potential misuse for social control.

4. Autonomous Weapons and the Loss of Human Control:

While still in development, autonomous weapons systems that can select and engage targets raise grave ethical concerns about removing human judgment from warfare and the potential for unintended consequences.

5. AI-Powered Facial Recognition in Public Spaces:

Ubiquitous facial recognition technology, used for surveillance and identification, raises concerns about mass data collection, privacy violations, and potential misuse for profiling and discrimination.

6. Emotion Recognition Software and Workplace Monitoring:

Tools claiming to "read" facial expressions and emotions pose ethical concerns for their accuracy, potential for manipulation, and the chilling effect of constant employee monitoring.

7. Algorithmic Manipulation of Social Media Feeds:

Social media platforms using AI algorithms to personalize content can create echo chambers, filter bubbles, and manipulate users' political views or purchasing decisions, raising concerns about freedom of information and informed choices.

8. AI-Generated Propaganda and Disinformation:

Malicious actors can exploit AI to create convincing fake news articles, manipulate images and videos, and spread misinformation at scale, undermining trust in media and democratic processes.

9. Algorithmic Trading and Market Manipulation:

High-frequency trading algorithms exploiting loopholes and manipulating markets raise concerns about unfair advantages, market instability, and potential harm to investors.

10. Overreliance on AI in Healthcare and Missing the Human Touch:

While AI can assist in diagnosis and treatment, overreliance on algorithms can overlook crucial human aspects like empathy, intuition, and ethical considerations, potentially harming patients and compromising the doctor-patient relationship.

These examples showcase the potential downsides of AI when ethical and legal boundaries are overstepped. They underscore the importance of responsible development, transparent algorithms, human oversight, and robust regulations to ensure AI serves humanity for good.

AI is a powerful tool with incredible potential, but it must be wielded responsibly. The examples above serve as a stark reminder of the dangers of unchecked AI development and deployment. By learning from these instances, we can ensure that AI advances ethically, upholds human values, and contributes to a more just and equitable society. We must remember that AI is not inherently good or bad; it reflects the values and intentions of its creators. Our choices today will shape how AI impacts our future. Let us choose wisely.

Chapter FOUR

Legal Frameworks for governing generative AI.

Legal frameworks for governing generative AI can be adapted from existing frameworks, such as sector-specific regulations and risk-based regulation. Global collaboration and regulatory sandboxes can also be utilized to address the challenges and considerations of regulating generative.[37]

Moreover, the use of ethical guidelines and principles can also aid in regulating generative AI. The IEEE Global Initiative for Ethical Considerations in AI and Autonomous Systems has developed a set of ethical principles that can be applied to the development and deployment of AI systems, including generative AI.[38] These principles include transparency, accountability, and privacy, among others. By adhering to these principles, developers and

37 Dubber, Pasquale and Das (n 3).

38 'The IEEE Global Initiative on Ethics of Autonomous and Intelligent Systems' (*IEEE Standards Association*) <https://standards.ieee.org/industry-connections/ec/autonomous-systems/> accessed 13 February 2024.

regulators can ensure that generative AI is developed and used in a responsible and ethical manner.

It is crucial to recognize that the ethical implications of AI extend beyond its technical capabilities. As AI technology becomes more advanced and integrated into society, it has the potential to impact various aspects of our lives. Therefore, it is essential to consider robust Legal frameworks that regulates AI throughout its entire lifecycle, from development to deployment. As stated by Floridi and Cowls[39], "AI ethics should be integrated into the design process from the outset, rather than being an afterthought or bolt-on".[40] By doing so, we can ensure that generative AI is developed and used in a way that aligns with societal values and promotes the greater good.

Collaboration is crucial when designing AI systems. It is essential to involve ethicists and policymakers in the development of generative AI to ensure that it is used in a responsible and ethical manner. For instance, when generative AI is used to develop personalized treatment plans for patients based on their medical history and

39 Luciano Floridi and Josh Cowls, 'A Unified Framework of Five Principles for AI in Society' (2019) 1 Harvard Data Science Review <https://hdsr.mitpress.mit.edu/pub/l0jsh9d1/release/8> accessed 13 February 2024.

40 Luciano Floridi and Josh Cowls, 'A Unified Framework of Five Principles for AI in Society' (2019) 1 Harvard Data Science Review <https://hdsr.mitpress.mit.edu/pub/l0jsh9d1/release/8> accessed 13 February 2024.

genetic makeup. It is important to include other healthcare professionals, including getting the patient's informed consent. The development of AI should be guided by ethical principles that prioritize human well-being and respect for human rights".

What legal frameworks can we weave to foster innovation while safeguarding our ethical compass? The following are five potential legal basis upon which we can build legal structures to help us navigate the treacherous terrain between progress and precaution.

Adapting Existing Frameworks.

The legal landscape, though not built with AI in mind, already possesses tools relevant to generative AI's challenges. Existing frameworks on copyright, data protection, and consumer protection can offer a starting point. The UK's Copyright, Designs and Patents Act 1988 grapples with AI authorship, while the Data Protection Act 2018 and GDPR safeguard personal data used in AI training. However, these frameworks, designed for a pre-AI era, require adaptation to effectively address the nuances of generative outputs and algorithmic decision-making.

Sector-Specific Regulations: Recognizing the limitations of generic frameworks, some countries are venturing into sector-specific regulations. The EU's proposed AI Act[41], for instance, focuses on high-risk AI applications like facial recognition and deepfakes, demanding transparency and human oversight. This tailored approach, though promising, needs careful consideration to avoid stifling innovation in less risky realms.

Risk-Based Regulation: Another potential framework is risk-based regulation, where the level of regulatory intensity scales with the potential harm an AI application poses. This approach, championed by the UK government, could offer flexibility while ensuring adequate safeguards for high-risk domains. However, accurately assessing and classifying risk remains a challenge, requiring collaboration between legal experts, technologists, and ethicists.

Global Collaboration: The challenge of governing generative AI is transnational. As AI applications transcend national borders, international cooperation is crucial. Efforts like the OECD's Principles on Artificial Intelligence aim to establish global ethical guidelines and promote standardized regulations. Collaborative approaches like these are essential to prevent a regulatory patchwork that could hinder innovation and harm consumers.

---

41 'EU AI Act: First Regulation on Artificial Intelligence | Topics | European Parliament' (11:40:00.0) <https://www.europarl.europa.eu/topics/en/article/20230601STO93804/eu-ai-act-first-regulation-on-artificial-intelligence> accessed 16 February 2024.

Regulatory Sandboxes: To foster responsible AI development while mitigating risks, the concept of "regulatory sandboxes" is gaining traction. These sandboxes provide controlled environments for testing and experimenting with AI applications under regulatory supervision. This experimental space allows for learning and adaptation, enabling regulators to develop effective frameworks without stifling innovation.

Building a robust legal framework for generative AI is no easy feat. There will be challenges like balancing innovation and precaution. Defining "*harm*" in the context of AI and ensuring enforceability will need careful consideration. Furthermore, public engagement and education are crucial for building trust and acceptance of the legal framework's legitimacy.

Designing a new legal landscape for governing AI has never been necessary. With careful consideration of existing frameworks, sector-specific regulations, risk-based approaches, global collaboration, and innovative solutions like regulatory sandboxes, we can strive for a future where legal structures nurture responsible AI development and protect societal well-being. We must be reminded that navigating the legal complexities of generative AI is not merely a technical undertaking; it is a social and ethical imperative. By engaging in open dialogue, embracing innovation responsibly, and upholding ethical principles, we can craft a legal framework that fosters a flourishing generative future, where creativity thrives in harmony with responsible governance.

Chapter FIVE

Redefining Intelligence - Beyond Benchmarks and Games.

For decades, the public perception of intelligence has been heavily influenced by media portrayals of supercomputers mastering chess boards and robots trouncing Go champions. While these achievements are undoubtedly impressive, they represent a narrow and limiting view of what intelligence truly is. It's time we move beyond benchmarks and games, recognizing the rich tapestry of human intelligence and the dangers of equating it with its artificial counterpart.

It is important to acknowledge that intelligence is a complex and multifaceted concept that cannot be fully captured by standardized tests or computer algorithms According to Gardner's theory of multiple intelligences, there are at least eight different types of intelligence, including linguistic, logical-mathematical, spatial, musical, bodily-kinesthetic, interpersonal, intrapersonal, and naturalistic.[42] Each of these intelligences involves a unique set of skills

42 Gavriel Salomon, *Distributed Cognitions: Psychological and Educational Considerations* (Cambridge University Press 1997).

and abilities that can be developed and applied in various contexts. Therefore, it is crucial to recognize the diversity of human intelligence and avoid reducing it to a single measure or metric.

The Tyranny of Benchmarks.

Imagine judging the intellectual prowess of a musician by their ability to solve calculus problems. As absurd as those sounds, it reflects the fundamental flaw in equating intelligence with performance on specific, pre-defined tasks. Games like chess and go, while complex, operate within rigidly defined rules and objectives. They prioritize pattern recognition, logical deduction, and optimal decision-making within those constraints. While these are valuable cognitive skills, they are merely a subset of what constitutes human intelligence.

Here's why relying solely on benchmarks falls short:

- Limited Scope: Focusing on specific tasks ignores the vast spectrum of human abilities, from emotional intelligence and social awareness to creativity, adaptability, and practical problem-solving. Can an AI system write a heartfelt, empathetic novel written to communicate a friend's grief, or navigate the nuances of social interaction? The jury is out on that one.

- Context is Key: Human intelligence thrives in dynamic, often messy environments. We process information, make decisions, and adapt to circumstances beyond pre-programmed rules. Benchmarks lack the context and real-world complexity that defines human thought and action.
- Evolution, Not Static State: True intelligence is not a fixed score but an ongoing process of learning, growing, and adapting to new information and situations. Benchmarks capture a snapshot of performance, not the dynamic nature of human cognitive development.

The Symphony of Human Intelligence:

Human intelligence is a beautiful symphony, everyone playing a unique instrument, contributing to the richness of the whole. Let us consider the diverse forms of intelligence that flourish around us:

- Social Intelligence: Navigating complex social dynamics, understanding emotions, and building meaningful relationships are hallmarks of human interaction, skills demonstrably absent in current AI.
- Emotional Intelligence: Empathy, self-awareness, and the ability to manage emotions

are crucial for navigating the human experience, areas where AI still struggles.

- Creative Intelligence: From composing music to inventing new technologies, human creativity pushes boundaries and fuels progress. Whilst AI can write a novel, it cannot capture the human condition within the pages, or paint a masterpiece that evokes deep emotions? Not yet at least. Perhaps it may be able to do so in the near future when there is enough data to inform it.
- Practical Intelligence: Solving everyday problems, adapting to new situations, and using common sense are essential for navigating the world, areas where AI systems are still under development.

This list is not exhaustive, but it highlights the vastness and depth of human intelligence that extend far beyond game-playing prowess.

The Difference Between Artificial and Human Intelligence.

The main difference between artificial and human intelligence is that AI is programmed to perform specific tasks and can probably outperform human on repetitive tasks, however human intelligence is based on experience, intuition, and creativity. Human intelligence allows us to understand complex situations, make nuanced decisions, and adapt to new circumstances. AI, on the other hand, is limited by its programming and cannot replicate these abilities. Common sense reasoning is essentially where we differ. While humans can make intuitive decisions based on their experiences, AI must continue to rely on algorithms and data analysis. This means that AI may not be able to make intuitive decisions or understand situations that require common sense reasoning.

For example, if an AI system is designed to identify objects in an image, it may not be able to recognize the context in which those objects are placed. This means that it may not be able to identify objects that are partially hidden or obscured by other objects.

The Challenge of Understanding Emotions and Social Cues.

Another limitation of AI is its inability to understand human emotions and social cues. While humans can interpret facial expressions, tone of voice, and body language to understand how someone is feeling, AI relies on algorithms and data analysis.

This means that AI may not be able to recognize sarcasm or irony in language or understand the emotional context of a situation. This can lead to misinterpretations or incorrect decisions based on incomplete information.

AI also struggles with understanding abstract concepts and creativity. While humans can imagine new ideas or concepts based on their experiences and knowledge, AI is limited by its programming.

This means that AI may not be able to come up with new ideas or solutions that have not been programmed into it.

The Limitations of Machine Learning and Data Bias.

Machine learning algorithms are a key component of many AI systems. However, these algorithms are only as good as the data they are trained on. If the data used to train an algorithm is biased or incomplete, the algorithm will also be biased or incomplete.

This means that AI systems may perpetuate existing biases or discrimination if they are trained on biased data. It also means that AI systems may not be able to make accurate predictions if they are trained on incomplete data.

The Risks of Overreliance on AI and Automation.

AI undoubtedly has many benefits without question however there are risks associated with overreliance on automation. If we rely too heavily on AI systems without human oversight or intervention, we run the risk of catastrophic consequences if something goes wrong. For example, in the cases of self-driving car malfunctions without a human driver present, this could cause a serious accident.

The Importance of Human Oversight and Intervention.

Human oversight and intervention are crucial when it comes to using AI systems in various industries. While AI can perform specific tasks more efficiently than humans in some cases, it still requires human judgment and ethical considerations.

Human oversight can help ensure that AI systems are making ethical decisions and avoiding biased or discriminatory outcomes. It can also help ensure that there is a backup plan in case something goes wrong with an automated system.

Finally, the challenge of adapting to new situations and unforeseen circumstances is another limitation of AI. While it may be able to perform well in a controlled environment, it may struggle when faced with unexpected challenges or changes in its environment.

Despite these limitations, AI still has enormous potential to transform our world for the better. However, it is important that we approach this technology with realistic expectations and recognize that human oversight and intervention will always be necessary. By doing so, we can ensure that AI is used responsibly and ethically to benefit society.

To make AI legal and humble. It is crucial to communicate to the technological world to appreciate the complexities of human intelligence. To build AI systems that understands their limitations, recognises, and values the diverse facets of human cognitive abilities. They must go beyond understanding intelligence as only in the realm of logical reasoning and analytical skills. Understanding Intelligence must encompass emotional intelligence, the capacity to empathise, and the ability to navigate the intricacies of human relationships. Moreover, the adaptability of the human mind is a testament to its intelligence. The ability to learn, unlearn, and relearn is a distinctive feature that sets human intelligence apart. In the rapidly changing landscape of technology, where algorithms evolve at a staggering pace, humans too must adapt to be able to navigate the complexities of the modern world.

Chapter SIX

Laws Requiring re-enactment in the Age of AI.

The rapid advancement of artificial intelligence (AI) presents exciting opportunities, but also throws a wrench into the established legal frameworks of countries like the UK and the US. Existing laws, crafted in an era without self-driving cars, facial recognition software, or AI-powered stock traders, are struggling to keep pace with the ethical and legal complexities posed by this new technology. Let's explore 20 areas where the law needs revision and analyse the potential impact of AI on key legal domains:

Areas requiring re-enactment.

1. Liability and Responsibility:

- Who is responsible for an AI's actions? The programmer, the manufacturer, the user, or a combination? Current product liability laws may not adequately address AI-caused harm, requiring clearer guidelines and potential shared responsibility models.

- Criminal culpability for AI systems? Can an AI be held criminally responsible for its actions, or should liability solely fall on humans involved in its development and deployment?

The question of responsibility in the event of AI errors or accidents prompts a reconsideration of liability laws, defining the boundaries of accountability for both developers and users. It is necessary to establishing clear legal frameworks for liability and responsibility in accidents involving self-driving cars.

2. Data Privacy and Ownership:

- Who owns the data used to train AI systems? Is it the data provider, the AI developer, or a shared ownership model? Existing data privacy laws might need adjustments to address anonymization, aggregation, and secondary use of data for AI training.
- Algorithmic bias and discrimination: How can we ensure fairness and prevent discriminatory outcomes in AI-driven decision-making systems? Robust regulations are needed to

address potential biases in data, algorithms, and deployment.

The exponential growth in data generation and utilization necessitates a re-evaluation of existing data protection laws to address the unique challenges posed by AI-driven analytics and processing. The invasion of privacy by AI systems calls for a stringent reassessment of privacy regulations, ensuring that individuals are safeguarded from unwarranted intrusions into their personal lives.

3. Intellectual Property Rights:

- Who owns AI-generated creations? Should the AI, its programmer, or the user hold intellectual property rights for inventions, art, or writing produced by AI systems? New frameworks are needed to address authorship, ownership, and potential licensing models.
- Copyright implications of AI-generated content: Can AI-created content be copyrighted, and if so, who holds the copyright? Existing copyright laws might need modifications to address ownership and infringement issues related to AI-generated works.

The dynamic nature of AI-generated content demands a nuanced approach to intellectual property laws, striking a balance between innovation and the protection of creators' rights.

4. Employment Laws and the Changing Nature of Work:

- Who are "employees" in the age of AI? Do AI-powered robots deserve worker protections, and how will automation affect existing labour laws and regulations? Redefining "employee" and adjusting labour laws might be necessary to address issues like minimum wage, working hours, and safety regulations for AI-powered systems.
- Job displacement due to AI: How can we ensure a just transition for workers displaced by automation? Retraining programs, social safety nets, and potential universal basic income models might need consideration.

As AI systems increasingly encroach upon traditional job roles, employment laws must adapt to address issues such as job displacement, retraining, and the ethical treatment of AI-assisted workers.

5. Criminal Laws:

- The potential misuse of AI in the commission of cybercrimes necessitates updates to criminal laws, ensuring that legal systems are equipped to handle novel forms of criminal activities facilitated by advanced technologies. For example, in the cases of Weaponized AI. We should consider developing Laws that will prevent the development and use of autonomous weapons systems.

6. Bias and Discrimination in AI Algorithms:

- Identifying and mitigating algorithmic bias: How can we prevent AI systems from perpetuating or amplifying societal biases based on race, gender, or other factors? Should AI systems be as culpable as humans when they perpetuate bias? Robust regulations and oversight mechanisms are crucial to ensure fairness and non-discrimination in AI applications.
- Transparency and explainability of AI decisions: How can we understand how AI systems reach their decisions, especially in high-stakes areas like loan approvals or criminal justice? Explainable AI frameworks are needed

to ensure accountability and prevent discriminatory outcomes.

With AI systems susceptible to biases, laws must explicitly address and regulate discriminatory practices, ensuring fairness and equity in algorithmic decision-making.

7. Consumer Protection Laws:

AI-driven products and services require enhanced consumer protection measures to safeguard against deceptive practices, biased algorithms, and inadequate transparency. With the increasing use of artificial intelligence (AI) in various industries, including finance, healthcare, and retail, there is a growing concern about the potential risks and harms that AI-powered products and services may pose to consumers. As AI becomes more prevalent in our daily lives, it is crucial to ensure that consumer protection laws are updated and adapted to address the unique challenges posed by this technology. According to a study by the European Parliament, "the development of AI raises important ethical, legal and societal questions that require a comprehensive regulatory framework." [43]

Furthermore, the potential impact of AI on employment and the economy is a growing concern. A report by the

43 'European Parliament Resolution of 16 February 2017 with Recommendations to the Commission on Civil Law Rules on Robotics (2015/2103(INL))'.

McKinsey Global Institute estimates that up to 800 million jobs could be displaced by automation by 2030, with low-skilled workers being particularly vulnerable.[44] This highlights the need for policymakers to not only address the ethical and legal implications of AI, but also to consider its broader societal implications.

8. Antitrust Laws:

The concentration of AI capabilities in the hands of a few tech giants prompts a reassessment of antitrust laws to prevent monopolistic practices that stifle competition and innovation. Antitrust laws are designed to promote competition and prevent monopolies in the market concerns have been raised about the potential for AI to create or reinforce monopolies. As AI becomes more prevalent in various industries, it is important to consider how antitrust laws can be applied to ensure fair competition. According to a study by the Stanford Institute for Human-Centered Artificial Intelligence, "AI and Antitrust: A Comprehensive Framework," antitrust laws should be updated to address the unique challenges posed by AI.

9. Healthcare Laws:

Artificial intelligence (AI) has the potential to revolutionize healthcare by improving patient outcomes, reducing

44 Manyika and others (n 26).

costs, and increasing efficiency. However, the use of AI in healthcare also raises legal and ethical concerns. As AI becomes more prevalent in healthcare, it is important to consider how existing laws and regulations apply to this technology and whether new laws are needed to address its unique challenges. For example, issues related to data privacy, liability, and bias must be carefully considered when implementing AI in healthcare settings.[45]

These concerns must be addressed to ensure that AI is used ethically and responsibly in healthcare. AI algorithms are only as unbiased as the data they are trained on, and if that data is biased, then the algorithm will be too .[46] This can lead to disparities in healthcare outcomes for different groups of people, particularly those from marginalized communities. To address this issue, it is important to ensure that the data used to train AI algorithms is diverse and representative of all populations.[47]

10. Environmental Laws:

The environmental impact of AI development and usage demands considerations within existing environmental laws, addressing issues such as energy consumption

---

45 Fei Jiang and others, 'Artificial Intelligence in Healthcare: Past, Present and Future' (2017) 2 Stroke and Vascular Neurology Artificial Intelligence <https://svn.bmj.com/content/2/4/230> accessed 13 February 2024.

46 Obermeyer and others (n 15).

47 Ibid

and electronic waste. AI can help in monitoring and predicting environmental changes, managing natural resources, and reducing pollution. However, the use of AI in environmental management raises legal and ethical concerns. The current environmental laws may not be sufficient to regulate the use of AI in this field. Therefore, there is a need for new laws and regulations that address the challenges posed by AI in environmental management. As AI systems become more complex and autonomous, it becomes increasingly difficult to determine who is responsible for their actions and decisions. This highlights the need for new legal frameworks that can address these issues and ensure that AI is used in a responsible and ethical manner .

11. National Security Laws:

National security laws are crucial in ensuring the safety and protection of a country's citizens. With the rise of artificial intelligence (AI), there is a growing concern about how these laws will be affected. As AI becomes more advanced, it may be used to carry out cyber-attacks or other malicious activities that could threaten national security. Therefore, it is important for policymakers to consider the implications of AI on national security laws and develop appropriate regulations to mitigate potential risks. [48]

48 'Download.Pdf' <https://bipartisanpolicy.org/download/?file=/wp-content/uploads/2020/07/BPC-Artificial-Intelligence-and-National-Security_Brief-Final-1.pdf> accessed 13 February 2024.

The ethical implications of AI in warfare are not limited to accountability and responsibility. According to a study by the Centre for a New American Security, the use of AI in military operations can also lead to unintended consequences such as civilian casualties and damage to critical infrastructure.[49] These consequences can have long-lasting effects on the affected communities and can undermine the legitimacy of military operations. Therefore, policymakers must consider the potential risks and benefits of AI in warfare and develop ethical guidelines to ensure its responsible use.

12. Education Laws:

According to a study by UNESCO, "the use of AI in education raises important ethical and legal questions that need to be addressed by policymakers" (UNESCO, 2019).[50] Laws and policies must be updated to address the use of AI in the classroom.

---

49 Paul Scharre and Michael C Horowitz, 'An Introduction to AUTONOMY in WEAPON SYSTEMS' (Center for a New American Security 2015) <https://www.jstor.org/stable/resrep06106> accessed 13 February 2024.

50 Francesc Pedro and others, 'Artificial Intelligence in Education : Challenges and Opportunities for Sustainable Development' [2019] MINISTERIO DE EDUCACIÓN <https://repositorio.minedu.gob.pe/handle/20.500.12799/6533> accessed 13 February 2024.

13. Robotics Laws:

The emergence of physical robots and autonomous systems requires specialized legislation to govern their interactions with humans, addressing issues of safety, liability, and ethical considerations. The field of robotics has already seen significant growth in recent years, with robots being used in a variety of industries, from manufacturing to healthcare. However, as robots become more autonomous and intelligent, there is a growing concern about their potential impact on society. To address these concerns, several countries have already implemented laws and guidelines for the development and use of robots. For example, the European Union has proposed a set of guidelines for ethical AI that includes principles such as transparency, accountability, and privacy.[51]

Similarly, Japan has established the Robot Revolution Realization Council to develop a roadmap for the future of robotics in the country, with a focus on safety, security, and privacy. [52] These efforts demonstrate a growing recognition of the need for responsible development and use of robots. However, there is still much work to be done to ensure that

---

51 'Ethics Guidelines for Trustworthy AI | Shaping Europe's Digital Future' (8 April 2019) <https://digital-strategy.ec.europa.eu/en/library/ethics-guidelines-trustworthy-ai> accessed 13 February 2024.

52 Anthony Fensom, 'Japan's Robot Revolution' <https://thediplomat.com/2015/07/japans-robot-revolution/> accessed 13 February 2024.

these guidelines are effectively implemented and enforced across industries and borders.

14. Transportation Laws:

The integration of artificial intelligence (AI) in transportation has the potential to revolutionize the way we move people and goods. However, as with any new technology, there are legal and regulatory challenges that must be addressed. Transportation laws will need to be updated to account for the unique characteristics of AI systems, such as their ability to learn and adapt to new situations. Additionally, liability issues will need to be clarified in the event of accidents involving autonomous vehicles. Despite these challenges, the benefits of AI in transportation are too great to ignore, and policymakers must work to create a legal framework that encourages innovation while ensuring public safety.[53]

15. Finance Laws:

The finance industry uses AI to automate tasks such as fraud detection, risk assessment, and investment management One of the main legal issues raised using AI in finance is the potential for discrimination. AI algorithms can perpetuate biases and discriminate against certain groups, such as minorities or women, if they are trained on biased data. This

53 Jasmin Bharadiya, 'Artificial Intelligence in Transportation Systems A Critical Review' (2023) 6 American Journal of Computing and Engineering 34.

can lead to unfair treatment and exclusion from financial services. To address this issue, regulators and financial institutions need to ensure that AI systems are transparent, explainable, and auditable, and that they are regularly monitored for bias and discrimination .[54]

16. Media and Entertainment Laws:

Media and entertainment industries are rapidly adopting artificial intelligence (AI) technologies to enhance their products and services. However, the use of AI in these industries raises legal and ethical concerns, particularly in relation to intellectual property rights, privacy, and liability. As AI becomes more prevalent in media and entertainment, it is important for lawmakers and industry stakeholders to address these issues to ensure that AI is used responsibly and ethically.

17. International Trade Laws:

As AI becomes more prevalent in trade, it raises important legal and regulatory questions. For example, how can countries ensure that AI-powered trade is fair and equitable? What are the implications of AI and can they be party to a contract? These questions are becoming increasingly urgent as AI continues to reshape the global economy. According to a report by the World Intellectual Property

54 Ibid

Organization (WIPO), "AI is poised to play an increasingly important role in international trade, and it is essential that policymakers and stakeholders work together to develop a legal framework that can support this new reality" (WIPO, 2019).[55]

18. Cybersecurity Laws:

The integration of AI into various industries has led to a growing concern about the security of sensitive data and the potential for cyber-attacks. In response, governments around the world are implementing cybersecurity laws and regulations to protect against these threats. These laws aim to establish guidelines for the development and use of AI, as well as provide legal consequences for those who violate them.[56]

Moreover, it is important to note that the consequences of violating these guidelines extend beyond legal repercussions. Non-compliance with data protection regulations can also result in reputational damage, loss of customer trust, and financial losses for businesses. In fact, a study by Ponemon Institute (2018) found that the average cost of a data breach for companies in the United States was $7.91 million. Therefore, it is crucial for organizations to prioritize data

55 Ibid

56 'Download.Pdf' (n 43).

protection and implement robust security measures to prevent breaches and ensure compliance with regulations.

19. Human Rights Laws:

Human rights laws are designed to protect individuals from discrimination, ensure equal treatment, and safeguard privacy. However, the use of AI can potentially violate these rights if not properly regulated and monitored. As such, there is a growing need for human rights laws to be updated and adapted to address the challenges posed by AI technology.

Moreover, improper development or misuse AI technology has the potential to exacerbate existing inequalities and discrimination in society. For example, biased algorithms can perpetuate racial and gender stereotypes, leading to unfair treatment and outcomes for certain groups. This highlights the importance of ensuring that AI systems are designed and implemented in a way that upholds human rights principles such as non-discrimination and equality. As noted by Floridi and Taddeo that 'the ethical challenges posed by AI require a new approach to human rights that takes into account the unique features of this technology'.[57]

57 Luciano Floridi and Mariarosaria Taddeo, 'What Is Data Ethics?' (2016) 374 Philosophical Transactions of the Royal Society A: Mathematical, Physical and Engineering Sciences 20160360.

20. Social media Laws:

The impact of AI on social media platforms requires a re-evaluation of laws governing online spaces, appropriate classification, correct warnings of the use of social media, appropriate age, also addressing issues such as content moderation, misinformation, and the ethical use of AI in influencing public discourse. Addressing the potential for AI-powered manipulation of social media and political discourse.

AI can be used to analyse user data and behaviour to personalize content and advertisements, but it can also be used to manipulate users or spread false information.[58]

It is crucial to establish guidelines for the ethical use of AI in social media platforms to prevent potential harm to users.

58 'Download.Pdf' (n 43).

Chapter SEVEN

The Philosophy of Humble AI - Complementing Humanity, Not Replacing It.

In the face of ever-evolving AI capabilities, a critical question emerges: what role should AI play in our future? Should it strive to emulate and potentially surpass human intelligence, or should it take a humbler approach, designed to complement, and augment our unique strengths? The concept of "Humble AI" proposes not a subservient machine, but one imbued with transparency, accountability, and a unwavering commitment to human oversight. It is a symphony of collaboration, where AI augments human creativity, not replaces it, where technology serves humanity, not the other way around.

Instead of viewing AI as a competitor, Humble AI embraces the following Core Principles namely.

- Transparency and Explainability: AI decisions should be transparent and understandable, allowing humans to assess their logic and reasoning. This prevents "black box" algorithms from perpetuating bias or making inexplicable choices.

- Human-Centred Design and Development: AI systems should be designed and developed with human needs and values in mind. This ensures they align with our ethical principles and serve humanity's best interests.
- Collaboration and Augmentation: Rather than aiming for replacement, Humble AI focuses on collaborating with humans and augmenting our capabilities. This creates a synergistic relationship where AI amplifies human strengths and overcomes our limitations.

By embracing these principles, we move beyond the dystopian fantasies of rogue machines and step into a future where humans and AI collaborate, learn from each other, and co-create a more just and equitable world. Imagine artists employing AI-powered tools to push the boundaries of their craft, not fearing displacement but embracing AI as a fellow creator. Doctors collaborating with AI-powered diagnostic tools, not to rely solely on algorithmic pronouncements, but to benefit from enhanced insight and data analysis. Educators partnering with AI tutors to personalize learning, not to automate education, but to empower each student to reach their full potential.

Real-World Examples of Humble AI:

The benefits of this philosophy extend far beyond theoretical discussions. Here are some real-world examples of how Humble AI can empower individuals and enhance society:

- **Personalized Education:** AI tutors can adapt to individual learning styles, offer targeted feedback, and identify areas needing improvement, while teachers provide crucial human guidance and emotional support.
- **Medical Diagnosis and Treatment:** AI algorithms can analyse large datasets to support doctors in early disease detection, treatment planning, and personalized medicine, while doctors maintain direct patient interaction and clinical judgment.
- **Climate Change Mitigation:** AI can analyse complex environmental data to predict weather patterns, optimize resource management, and identify areas most vulnerable to climate change, informing human-led efforts to combat the crisis.
- **Accessibility Tools**: AI-powered software can translate languages in real-time, transcribe speech to text, and generate audio descriptions of images, breaking down communication barriers and empowering individuals with

disabilities. An example is the invention of the headphone device which translates language in real-time helping people of diverse language communicate in real-time.

- **Creative Collaboration:** AI tools can assist artists and musicians in composing music, generating visuals, and exploring new creative possibilities, while human imagination and artistic expression remain at the core of the process.

These are just a few examples, but they illustrate the vast potential of Humble AI to improve lives, solve complex problems, and usher in a future where technology empowers, rather than displaces, humanity.

Moving forward, we must actively cultivate a culture of Humble AI. This requires collaboration between engineers, policymakers, ethicists, and the public to ensure AI development aligns with our shared values and benefits everyone. By fostering transparency, prioritizing human needs, and focusing on collaboration, we can leverage AI's power to create a more just, equitable, and prosperous future for all. Our participation in shaping the future where AI serves humanity is crucial.

Chapter EIGHT

Conclusion - Towards a Legally and Ethically Grounded Future with AI.

The tide of artificial intelligence is upon us, surging with transformative potential for every aspect of life. From reshaping industries to redefining communication, its impact will be undeniable. In this light, we stand at a crucial juncture. Do we succumb to the fear of the unknown and resist this inevitable wave, or do we proactively navigate it, ensuring AI complements and empowers humanity, not replaces, or controls it?

Inspiration from the Draft EU AI Act.

The European Union's draft AI Act[59] offers a valuable roadmap for legal frameworks adapted to the AI age. Key principles include:

59 'EU AI Act: First Regulation on Artificial Intelligence | Topics | European Parliament' (n 40).

- Risk-based approach: Categorizing AI applications based on their potential risk and applying stricter regulations to high-risk uses.
- Human oversight and explainability: Ensuring human oversight of critical AI systems and requiring explainability of AI decisions.
- Ban on certain high-risk uses: Prohibiting specific applications of AI deemed unethical or harmful, such as social scoring systems.

The legal landscape is in flux as we grapple with the implications of AI. By proactively revising existing laws and drawing inspiration from initiatives like the EU AI Act, we can ensure that AI develops responsibly and ethically, benefiting humanity without compromising our values and principles. It is important to note that this list is not exhaustive, and the conversation about adapting our legal frameworks to the AI age is just beginning. As AI continues to evolve, so too must our legal systems, ensuring a future where technology serves humanity, not the other way around.

The Singapore Model: Public Consultation on AI Impact.

In 2023, Singapore took a commendable step towards AI democratization by launching a public consultation on proposed "Advisory Guidelines on Use of Personal

Data in AI Recommendation and Decision Systems." [60] This initiative, inviting citizens to weigh in on how AI algorithms use personal data for tasks like loan approvals and medical diagnoses, serves as a shining example of public engagement in AI governance. By openly discussing anxieties around algorithmic fairness and data privacy, Singapore empowers its citizens to become co-creators of their AI future.

Public consultation is a start. To have a Legal and humble AI it must have the following features.

- **Accessibility:** Information presented in clear, easy-to-understand language, reaching beyond tech-savvy demographics.
- **Transparency:** Laying bare the workings of AI algorithms, demystifying the black box, and fostering trust.
- **Diversity:** Actively seeking out voices from marginalized communities, ensuring a plurality of perspectives informs AI development.
- **Actionable feedback:** Not just collecting opinions but incorporating them into concrete policy decisions and regulatory frameworks.

60 'EU AI Act: First Regulation on Artificial Intelligence | Topics | European Parliament' (n 44).

Shaping the Future.

By embracing public consultation and building bridges of informed engagement, we can create an "Orchestra of the Future" were citizens and AI play in harmony. Imagine a world where diverse voices shape AI development, where anxieties are addressed proactively, and where technology serves not as a dictator, but as a responsive instrument in the hands of a conscious electorate.

This is not just a utopian ideal; it is a necessity. As AI's footprint expands, so too must the democratic space for shaping its trajectory. We, the citizens, hold the notes that can compose a future of responsible, equitable, and human-cantered AI. Let us raise our voices, engage in the dialogue, and ensure that the public consultation becomes not just a fleeting melody, but an enduring chorus that guides the AI revolution towards a future we can all embrace.

Throughout this book, we have explored the vast spectrum of AI's potential, delving into its limitations, legal complexities, and ethical considerations. We have witnessed its remarkable capabilities in healthcare, and creative endeavours, while acknowledging the dangers of biases, algorithmic manipulation, and overstepping ethical boundaries.

The key takeaway is this: AI is not a monolith, nor is its future predetermined. The choices we make today, individually, and collectively, will shape its trajectory. This necessitates a multi-pronged approach:

1. Robust Legal Frameworks:

We must adapt existing legal structures to address the unique challenges posed by AI. Initiatives like the EU AI Act offer valuable blueprints, emphasizing transparency, explainability, human oversight, and risk-based regulations. These frameworks should evolve alongside AI, ensuring legal systems remain effective and ethical guardrails.

2. Ethical Principles in Development:

Building upon existing ethical frameworks like the Asilomar AI Principles and the Montreal Declaration for Responsible AI, we must establish clear ethical guidelines for AI development and deployment. These principles should prioritize human well-being, fairness, non-discrimination, and accountability, preventing harm and fostering beneficial AI applications.

3. Public Education and Engagement:

Open discussions about AI are crucial. Educating the public on its capabilities, limitations, and potential impacts empowers individuals to engage in informed discourse and participate in shaping AI's future. Transparency and accessibility are key to building trust and preventing fear-mongering narratives.

4. International Collaboration:

The challenges and opportunities presented by AI are global. International collaboration between governments, researchers, and civil society organizations is essential to establish shared ethical principles, harmonize legal frameworks, and ensure responsible development and deployment across borders.

5. Continuous Reassessment and Adaptation:

AI is a rapidly evolving field, demanding constant monitoring and adaptation. We must remain vigilant, reassessing ethical and legal frameworks regularly to address emerging challenges and ensure they remain relevant and effective.

This journey towards a responsible and beneficial future with AI will not be easy. It will require collaboration, open dialogue, and a commitment to upholding human values. Let us remember that AI is a tool, and like any tool, its impact depends on the hands that wield it. Let us choose wisely, ensuring that AI becomes a force for good, augmenting our capabilities and creating a brighter future for all.

We must remember, the most crucial element in this journey is You and me. We all have a role to play. No one wants a future created by AI that we do not want to be part of. It is important to engage in specific ways, such as contacting your local representatives, supporting relevant organizations, or participating in online forums.

By taking an active role in shaping the discourse and understanding the implications of AI, we can collectively steer this powerful technology towards a future that benefits all humanity.

BIBLIOGRAPHY

'Ai_index_2019_report.Pdf' <https://hai.stanford.edu/sites/default/files/ai_index_2019_report.pdf> accessed 13 February 2024

Bharadiya J, 'Artificial Intelligence in Transportation Systems A Critical Review' (2023) 6 American Journal of Computing and Engineering 34

Buolamwini J and Gebru T, 'Gender Shades: Intersectional Accuracy Disparities in Commercial Gender Classification', *Proceedings of the 1st Conference on Fairness, Accountability and Transparency* (PMLR 2018) <https://proceedings.mlr.press/v81/buolamwini18a.html> accessed 13 February 2024

Davenport T and Kalakota R, 'The Potential for Artificial Intelligence in Healthcare' (2019) 6 Future Healthcare Journal 94

'Download.Pdf' <https://bipartisanpolicy.org/download/?file=/wp-content/uploads/2020/07/BPC-Artificial-Intelligence-and-National-Security_Brief-Final-1.pdf> accessed 13 February 2024

Dressel J and Farid H, 'The Accuracy, Fairness, and Limits of Predicting Recidivism' (2018) 4 Science

Advances eaao5580

Dubber MD, Pasquale F and Das S, *The Oxford Handbook of Ethics of AI* (Oxford university press 2020)

'Data Protection Act 2018' <https://www.legislation.gov.uk/ukpga/2018/12/contents/enacted> accessed 21 February 2024

'EU AI Act: First Regulation on Artificial Intelligence | Topics | European Parliament' (11:40:00.0) <https://www.europarl.europa.eu/topics/en/article/20230601STO93804/eu-ai-act-first-regulation-on-artificial-intelligence> accessed 16 February 2024

Floridi L and Cowls J, 'A Unified Framework of Five Principles for AI in Society' (2019) 1 Harvard Data Science Review <https://hdsr.mitpress.mit.edu/pub/l0jsh9d1/release/8> accessed 13 February 2024

Lamensch M, 'Generative AI Tools Are Perpetuating Harmful Gender Stereotypes' (*Centre for International Governance Innovation*) <https://www.cigionline.org/articles/generative-ai-tools-are-perpetuating-harmful-gender-stereotypes/> accessed 16 February 2024

'Privacy Management Among Social Media Natives: An Exploratory Study of Facebook and Snapchat - Erin E. Hollenbaugh, 2019' <https://journals.

sagepub.com/doi/full/10.1177/2056305119855144> accessed 16 February 2024

'Regulation - 2016/679 - EN - Gdpr - EUR-Lex' <https://eur-lex.europa.eu/eli/reg/2016/679/oj> accessed 21 February 2024

'Report on Algorithmic Risk Assessment Tools in the U.S. Criminal Justice System' (*Partnership on AI*, 23 April 2019) <https://partnershiponai.org/paper/report-on-machine-learning-in-risk-assessment-tools-in-the-u-s-criminal-justice-system/> accessed 16 February 2024

'Sadiq Khan Says Fake AI Audio of Him Nearly Led to Serious Disorder' *BBC News* (13 February 2024) <https://www.bbc.com/news/uk-68146053> accessed 16 February 2024

Salomon G, *Distributed Cognitions: Psychological and Educational Considerations* (Cambridge University Press 1997)

'The Future of Jobs Report 2018' (*World Economic Forum*) <https://www.weforum.org/publications/the-future-of-jobs-report-2018/> accessed 13 February 2024

'What Are Autonomous Car Levels? Levels 1 to 5 of Driverless Vehicle Tech Explained' (*CAR Magazine*) <https://www.carmagazine.co.uk/car-news/tech/autonomous-car-levels-different-

driverless-technology-levels-explained/> accessed 21 February 2024

'GDPR_FINAL_EPSU.Pdf' <https://www.epsu.org/sites/default/files/article/files/GDPR_FINAL_EPSU.pdf> accessed 13 February 2024

'Getting the Future Right – Artificial Intelligence and Fundamental Rights' (*European Union Agency for Fundamental Rights*, 18 November 2020) <http://fra.europa.eu/en/publication/2020/artificial-intelligence-and-fundamental-rights> accessed 13 February 2024

Goodman B and Flaxman S, 'European Union Regulations on Algorithmic Decision-Making and a "Right to Explanation"' (2017) 38 AI Magazine 50

Grother P, Ngan M and Hanaoka K, 'Face Recognition Vendor Test Part 3:: Demographic Effects' (National Institute of Standards and Technology 2019) NIST IR 8280 <https://nvlpubs.nist.gov/nistpubs/ir/2019/NIST.IR.8280.pdf> accessed 13 February 2024

Gussek L and Wiesche M, 'The Gig Economy: Workers, Work and Platform Perspective' (2021)

Hildebrandt M and O'Hara K (eds), *Life and the Law in the Era of Data-Driven Agency* (Edward Elgar Publishing 2020)

'Independent-Work-Choice-Necessity-and-the-Gig-Economy-Full-Report.Pdf' <http://dln.jaipuria.ac.in:8080/jspui/bitstream/123456789/2851/1/Independent-Work-Choice-necessity-and-the-gig-economy-Full-report.pdf> accessed 13 February 2024

Jiang F and others, 'Artificial Intelligence in Healthcare: Past, Present and Future' (2017) 2 Stroke and Vascular Neurology <https://svn.bmj.com/content/2/4/230> accessed 13 February 2024

Lamensch M, 'Generative AI Tools Are Perpetuating Harmful Gender Stereotypes' (*Centre for International Governance Innovation*) <https://www.cigionline.org/articles/generative-ai-tools-are-perpetuating-harmful-gender-stereotypes/> accessed 16 February 2024

'Privacy Management Among Social Media Natives: An Exploratory Study of Facebook and Snapchat - Erin E. Hollenbaugh, 2019' <https://journals.sagepub.com/doi/full/10.1177/2056305119855144> accessed 16 February 2024

'Report on Algorithmic Risk Assessment Tools in the U.S. Criminal Justice System' (*Partnership on AI*, 23 April 2019) <https://partnershiponai.org/paper/report-on-machine-learning-in-risk-assessment-tools-in-the-u-s-criminal-justice-system/> accessed 16 February 2024

Lin K-Y and Lu H-P, 'Why People Use Social Networking Sites: An Empirical Study Integrating Network Externalities and Motivation Theory' (2011) 27 Computers in Human Behavior 1152

Manyika J and others, 'Jobs Lost, Jobs Gained: What the Future of Work Will Mean for Jobs, Skills, and Wages' (McKinsey Global Institute 2017) Report <https://apo.org.au/node/199751> accessed 13 February 2024

'Netflix's "The Great Hack" Highlights Cambridge Analytica's Role in Trinidad & Tobago Elections' (*Global Voices Advox*, 6 August 2019) <https://advox.globalvoices.org/2019/08/06/netflixs-the-great-hack-highlights-cambridge-analyticas-role-in-trinidad-tobago-elections/> accessed 13 February 2024

Obermeyer Z and others, 'Dissecting Racial Bias in an Algorithm Used to Manage the Health of Populations' (2019) 366 Science 447

OECD, 'An OECD Learning Framework 2030' in Gerald Bast, Elias G Carayannis and David FJ Campbell (eds), *The Future of Education and Labor* (Springer International Publishing 2019) <https://doi.org/10.1007/978-3-030-26068-2_3> accessed 13 February 2024

Pedro F and others, 'Artificial Intelligence in

Education : Challenges and Opportunities for Sustainable Development' [2019] MINISTERIO DE EDUCACIÓN <https://repositorio.minedu.gob.pe/handle/20.500.12799/6533> accessed 13 February 2024

Philip B, 'Artificial Intelligence Ante Portas: Legal & Ethical Reflections'

Russell S and Norvig P, *Artificial Intelligence: A Modern Approach, Global Edition* (3rd edition, Pearson 2016)

'Sadiq Khan Says Fake AI Audio of Him Nearly Led to Serious Disorder' *BBC News* (13 February 2024) <https://www.bbc.com/news/uk-68146053> accessed 16 February 2024

Salomon G, *Distributed Cognitions: Psychological and Educational Considerations* (Cambridge University Press 1997)

Scharre P and Horowitz MC, 'An Introduction to AUTONOMY in WEAPON SYSTEMS' (Center for a New American Security 2015) <https://www.jstor.org/stable/resrep06106> accessed 13 February 2024

'The Future of Jobs Report 2018' (*World Economic Forum*) <https://www.weforum.org/publications/the-future-of-jobs-report-2018/> accessed 13 February 2024

'The Ethics of Algorithms: Mapping the Debate - Brent Daniel Mittelstadt, Patrick Allo, Mariarosaria Taddeo, Sandra Wachter, Luciano Floridi, 2016' <https://journals.sagepub.com/doi/full/10.1177/2053951716679679> accessed 13 February 2024

'The Future of Jobs Report 2018' (*World Economic Forum*) <https://www.weforum.org/publications/the-future-of-jobs-report-2018/> accessed 13 February 2024

'The Future of Work: How New Technologies Are Transforming Tasks' (*MIT-IBM Watson AI Lab*) <https://mitibmwatsonailab.mit.edu/research/blog/the-future-of-work-how-new-technologies-are-transforming-tasks/> accessed 13 February 2024

'The IEEE Global Initiative on Ethics of Autonomous and Intelligent Systems' (*IEEE Standards Association*) <https://standards.ieee.org/industry-connections/ec/autonomous-systems/> accessed 13 February 2024

WIPO, 'WIPO Technology Trends 2019 - Artificial Intelligence' <https://www.wipo.int/publications/en/details.jsp?id=4396> accessed 13 February 2024

Cases

Donoghue v Stevenson [1932] UKHL 100 (UKHL (1932))

Montgomery v Lanarkshire Health Board [2015] UKSC 11 (UKSC (2015))

Nettleship v Weston [1971] EWCA Civ 6 (EWCA (Civ))

Legislation

Highway Act 1980

Road Traffic Act 1988

Data Protection Act 2018

Automated and Electric Vehicles Act 2018

EU General Data Protection Regulation 2016

Other titles written by the author

- Funny money.
- All white jury.
- Happiness manual.
- 7 Pillars of Great Leadership.
- The measure of a good man & woman.
- The weeping Leopard and Happy Baboon. (available in swahili).

Printed in Great Britain
by Amazon

38770234R00056